T0006415

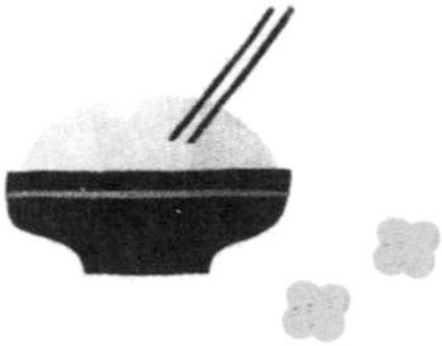

even cats & rice ladles

The wise and witty world of Japanese sayings

Text by Yoshie Omata

Illustrated by Nastia Sleptsova

Hardie Grant

QUADRILLE

Contents

Introduction 7

Flower snowstorm 10
Flower, bird, wind, moon 12
Sunlight leaking through trees 14
Cicadas drizzling 16
Small spring weather 18
Wilting trees 20
Silver world 22
Ten people, ten colours 24
Two people, three legs 26
Spirits go well together 28
Happy, angry, sad, fun 30
Praising your own painting 32
Single sword entering directly 34
Losing yourself in a dream 36
Through the heart, express the heart 38
Good luck comes at the gate of laughter 40
Spilt water cannot be put back into the bowl 42
A wise hawk hides its talons 44
It is darkest at the foot of the lighthouse 46
Specks of dust eventually make a mountain 48
If three people get together, excellent wisdom comes 50
The wind will blow again tomorrow 52
Very strong person under the floor 54
To cool the head 56
To stick your face out 58

To see with the long eye 60
The ear hurts 62
Teeth don't stand 64
To make the neck long 66
The hand comes out of the throat 68
To hold one's shoulder 70
To stretch out one's chest 72
The stomach stands 74
The waist is heavy 76
To carry the feet 78
To hang on the crotch 80
It doesn't fall into one's guts 82
The horse is a match 84
I wish to borrow even a cat's paw 86
Even cats and rice ladles 88
To read mackerel 90
Little fish grinding their teeth 92
The fish that you lost seems greater than it is 94
Even monkeys can fall down from trees 96
To swallow like a cormorant 98
A word from the crane 100
A line like a long snake 102
The moon and a soft-shell turtle 104
Dumplings over flowers 106
Packed like sushi 108

About the author 110

Introduction

Welcome to one small corner of the beautiful, subtle, complicated language that is Japanese. Perhaps you have picked up this book because you are learning Japanese, or maybe you are simply interested in discovering some of the more unusual aspects of the language. Whatever brought you here, you will find a fascinating selection of Japanese expressions, sayings and idioms to enjoy.

One of the most special elements of these expressions is how much they reveal about the culture and customs of Japan. It's not just about sushi, anime or tea ceremonies, and I hope that the sayings you learn in this book will help you to explore and appreciate many different aspects of Japanese culture.

Japan has a beautiful natural environment and four distinct seasons. Since ancient times in its islands, nature has played a crucial part of life and the people have always appreciated its beauty and subtlety. There are numerous proverbs inspired by the country's unique natural phenomena, and you will find many expressions that represent nature and the weather.

One peculiarity of the language is its idiomatic compound words, each consisting of four Chinese characters (known in Japanese as *kanji*), which are often used in daily conversations as well as in business settings. These phrases have a pleasant rhythm when you pronounce them, and lots of them express positive and encouraging messages that many people carry in their hearts as their mantras for life.

There are also plenty of Japanese sayings and proverbs that are succinct life lessons. From the long list of proverbs, I have selected the ones that seemed the most amusing, the most positive, and those that are reminiscent of the beauty of life.

Japanese people tend not to express private thoughts and feelings directly, but instead use a little creativity to show what is really on their minds. In this book you will find a collection of useful idioms that are spoken frequently by native speakers in daily conversations. Some of these expressions have clear parallels for English speakers, while others may sound unfamiliar. Hopefully all of them will make you smile.

For each expression, you will see the *romaji* (the Roman spelling) so you can learn the pronunciation. You will also find lots of charming illustrations, along with a translation explaining what each phrase means literally. The translations may sound a little unusual, but don't worry: there is an explanation for each one, telling you what it means and how it is used.

Let's get started!

Yoshie
@japanesewithyoshie

Flower snowstorm

HANA FUBUKI

花吹雪

Cherry blossom, or *sakura*, is well known for its short-lived and transient beauty. A gust of wind can easily lift the petals from the trees. The expression 花吹雪 / *hana fubuki* / evokes the delicate beauty of a shower of cherry blossom petals flying in the sky so thickly that it looks as if snow is falling. While many people think that cherry blossom petals are always pink, some kinds of cherry tree grow white petals, making the falling petals look like a soft snowstorm in spring.

Flower, bird, wind, moon

KACHOO FUUGETSU

花
鳥
風
月

This set of four Chinese characters literally represents flowers, birds, the wind and the moon. It encapsulates the beauty of nature and describes the natural features that Japanese people appreciate and enjoy in their surroundings. 花鳥風月 / *kachoo fuugetsu* / has also been used to describe the essential elements of Japanese aesthetics in paintings, songs, calligraphy and poetry. It can therefore be applied to things we enjoy in our daily lives, as well as the discoveries we make when we travel to different places.

Sunlight leaking through trees

KOMOREBI

木漏れ日

This expression consists of three words:

木 / *ko* / tree

漏れ / *more* / which is the verb stem of
漏れる / *moreru* / to leak or come through

日 / *bi* / day or sunlight.

It describes sunlight filtering through trees and as well as having a descriptive element, this saying is used to express a love of natural beauty. Let's imagine you walk into a forest on a sunny day and the light rays are filtering through the branches of leafy trees, the dappled sunlight reflected on the path. 木漏れ日 / *komorebi* / captures this very subtle and beautiful natural phenomenon in four short syllables. The concept does not really exist as a phrase in other languages and cannot be translated as a single word.

Cicadas
drizzling

SEMI SHIGURE

蝉
時
雨

This expression combines the words for cicadas and the drizzling rain of late autumn and early winter. The continuous chorus of cicadas is one of the main characteristics of local summertime, so it is associated with the arrival of hot and humid weather, which usually lasts from June to September. The sound of the cicadas singing signals that summer is coming, while reminding them of the sound of 時雨 / *shigure* / drizzling rain.

Small spring weather

KOHARU BIYORI

小春日和

When there is a spell of warm and dry
weather in late autumn or early winter,
at the transition between the two seasons,
Japanese people refer to a 'small spring'.
Much like 'Indian summer' in English, it
describes pleasant, calm and clear weather
that is enjoyed before the harshness of
winter fully arrives.

Wilting trees

KOGARASHI

木枯らし

A strong and biting wind blows away the last remaining leaves from the trees, which now droop, looking naked, cold and a little bit sad. In Japan, this wind blows between October and November, as if it is trying to remind us that winter is just around the corner. After losing their beautiful leaves, the trees seem to 'wilt' at the thought of the cold weather.

Silver world

GIN SEKAI

銀世界

Japan is a country where you can experience beautiful snowscapes in many places. The phrase 銀世界 / *gin sekai* / describes sunlight shining on the snow, creating a bright, white world. You may wonder why it is translated as silver and not white. In Japanese, there is a traditional colour scheme that has been passed down from ancient times. Since then, the subtle differences in colours of flowers and plants have been identified and given individual names. In the traditional Japanese colour scheme, silver can also mean white gold, which can translate as 'white which shines like silver'.

Ten people, ten colours

JUUNIN TOIRO

十人十色

Let's say there are ten people in a room. Their personalities, tastes, mindsets, values, beliefs, backgrounds and ways of doing things are all different: just like ten different colours, they are unique and cannot be interchanged. This saying proclaims that everyone is different and we should all be proud of our unique colours.

Two people, three legs

NININ SANKYAKU

二人三脚

When you work hard with someone and commit to achieving a mutual goal, it is very much like a three-legged race – running with your central legs tied together – where you both look in the same direction and try to synchronize your efforts. A pair might be work partners, a married couple, or a teacher and a student – any two people who work together. If a single person thinks they do not have enough strength to accomplish their goal, by combining efforts with another person they can support each other and make it happen, even if this means having to make compromises at times.

Spirits go well together

IKI TOOGOO

意気投合

Have you ever felt an instant connection with someone, to the point of wondering how you could ever have lived without them? That is when 'spirits go well together' in Japanese. This expression, similar to 'kindred spirits' in English, is used in situations where you meet someone for the first time and quickly realize that you both share the same values and interests, and immediately hit it off.

Happy, angry, sad, fun

KIDO AIRAKU

喜怒哀楽

The distinctive individual Chinese characters that make up this compound word represent the four cardinal feelings and emotions: happiness, anger, sadness and enjoyment. As human beings, our life experiences are hugely varied and evoke many different and complex emotions. This compound word expresses the whole gamut of those emotions in a simple, concise, yet effective way.

Praising your own painting

JIGA JISAN

自画自賛

One of the meanings of the Chinese character 画 is painting, but in this context, it denotes anything that you are proud of. Of course, it *could* be your own beautiful paintings, but it could equally be that you are proud of the products your company makes or proud of the way you have raised your children. 自画自賛 / *jiga jisan* / is when you want to praise your own work. While being humble is considered a good thing in Japanese culture, there is nothing wrong with feeling satisfaction and pride in your own achievements.

Single sword entering directly

TANTOO CHOKUNYUU

単刀直入

This phrase is used when a person gets straight to the point. In Japanese culture, talking directly or too straightforwardly can be considered impolite. However, there are times when it is appropriate to 'cut to the chase' and talk in a 単刀直入 / *tantoo chokunyuu* / way, saving time and energy. In Japan, you might still need to soften your direct statements with so-called 'cushion words' – 'Sorry to bother you but...', 'I am afraid to inform you that ...', 'I regret to tell you this but ...' – especially when you need to tone down awkward or disappointing topics, such as refusal or rejection, and compensate for being direct.

Losing yourself in a dream

MUGA MUCHUU

無我夢中

This compound word captures the moment when you are so absorbed in something that you lose yourself, maybe even forgetting where you are. It could be when you are reading a book from cover to cover in one go, or studying hard and realizing that hours have flown by while you are 'lost in thought'. For some people in our modern smartphone-centric world, focusing totally without being distracted can be quite a challenge, but if you have something in your life – a sport, a hobby or a passion – that can put you in a state of 無我夢中 / *muga muchuu* / it is a precious thing. The flipside of this is in hazardous situations when you need to direct the same focus to running for your life!

Through the heart, express the heart

ISHIN DENSHIN

以
心
伝
心

You think it is too cold in your office or lecture theatre, then the heating comes on without you asking for it. You are in the mood for bulgogi and your partner suggests you dine out at a Korean restaurant. When someone understands you without you saying a word, we call it 以心伝心 / *ishin denshin* /. Japanese culture relies heavily on context for subtleties of meaning, highlighting verbal communication in an indirect and sometimes ambiguous way – through tone, facial expression or gesture. Such non-verbal signals are important in overlaying words with additional nuances of meaning. But when you find someone who can understand you as if by telepathy, this is pure magic of the heart.

Good luck comes at the gate of laughter

WARAU KADO NI WA FUKU KITARU

笑う門には福来る

Here, the word 門 / *kado* / gate symbolizes home and family. This saying tells you that a happy family that smiles and laughs a lot attracts fortune and good luck. We all have to face difficulties at times in our lives, but if we look on the bright side and keep putting a smile on our face, so much more good luck will come our way.

Spilt water cannot be put back into the bowl

FUKUSUI BON NI KAERAZU

覆水盆に返らず

The English cry over spilt milk, but the Japanese cry over spilt water! The point is that what is done cannot be undone. In Japan, this saying also means that a couple that has split up will never get back together. This originates from an ancient Chinese legend, in which a wife leaves her husband but later tries to reconcile with him. He spills some water from a bowl and asks her to put it back into the bowl so that her wish can be fulfilled. Of course, she cannot do that, and the husband responds: 'spilt water cannot be put back into the bowl'.

A wise hawk hides its talons

NOO ARU TAKA WA TSUME O KAKUSU

能ある鷹は爪を隠す

Since ancient times, hawks – proud and majestic birds of prey – have been a symbol of excellence for the Japanese and a being to emulate in their restrained power. Like the hawk, a real person of talent does not show off their true abilities, while those with fewer abilities tend to talk too loudly and brag about their supposed knowledge and prowess.

It is darkest at the foot of the lighthouse

TOODAI MOTO KURASHI

灯台下暗し

Have you ever asked someone where your glasses were while you were actually wearing them? Have you ever come to appreciate all the positive aspects of your small home town after living in a big city? Or realized that there is so much more to enjoy in your environment when you welcome a visitor to your home? Just as lighthouses illuminate the distance while things close by remain in darkness, the things closest to us can often go unnoticed. But we can benefit by taking a closer look, because the darkness may be hiding something of value.

Specks of dust eventually make a mountain

CHIRI MO TSUMOREBA YAMA TO NARU

塵も積もれば山となる

Don't underestimate the small things, because when tiny things pile up, they can eventually turn into something huge. Such small things can, of course, be either positive or negative. If you put in a little effort every day towards a goal, then one day you will achieve something important. However, if you are wasting small amounts of time and money on a regular basis – even if they appear insignificant at first – it may result in tremendous loss in the long term. In modern Japanese, we use this saying in a shortened form: ちりつも / chiri-tsumo /. This sounds catchier and is often used to promote self help.

If three people get together, excellent wisdom comes

SANNIN YOREBA MONJU NO CHIE

On our own we may not be able to come up with astounding ideas, but if a few people get together and discuss their ideas, then they are likely to inspire each other to imagine some truly brilliant concepts. You don't have to sit alone scratching your head or try to puzzle out a problem on your own. Brainstorm with others, table your thoughts and take the best of them. English speakers may say that 'two heads are better than one' but this saying reminds us that three are even better!

三人寄れば文殊の知恵

The wind will blow again tomorrow

ASHITA WA ASHITA NO KAZE GA FUKU

Life gets difficult at times, and it is easy to feel disappointed or negative. But if you are feeling down today, take this Japanese expression to heart and listen to the flow of nature. Tomorrow is another day and the forces of nature will carry on regardless: what will be, will be. Stop worrying too much about what you cannot change.

明日は明日の風が吹く

Very strong person under the floor

EN NO SHITA NO CHIKARA MOCHI

縁の下の力持ち

If you work hard and put in all your efforts behind the scenes for the benefit of others, you are often described as being an unsung hero or heroine. 縁の下 / *en no shita* / means the space under the floor and refers to all those people who supply the support that others need to make the best of their lives, even if it means not getting any of the credit. We often focus on what is right in front of us but, in fact, that is actually only a small part of reality. This expression shines a spotlight on the unsung heroes whose satisfaction comes not from fame and glory but simply from making beautiful things happen, and lifting others to greater things.

To cool the head

ATAMA O HIYASU

頭を冷やす

This expression suggests that if you are irritated, angry or frustrated, you need to cool off and calm down. Of course, it's not actually advising you to put your head into ice-cold water! You can cool your head by taking a walk in the park with the dog, working out at the gym, spending time with your loved ones... anything that will prevent your inner machinery from overheating.

To stick your face out

KAO O DASU

顔を出す

When you pop in somewhere, the Japanese
say you 'stick your face out'. You can use this
idiom to tell someone who is organizing
a party that you cannot stay for long, yet still
plan to drop by and say hello, or when you
make a surprise visit to a clothing store where
your friend is working. In any situation where
you want to describe a brief or unexpected
visit, you can use this idiom.

To see with the long eye

NAGAI ME DE MIRU

長い目でみる

Life is full of surprises – some of them not so great – so sometimes it is a good idea to 'look at things with the long eye', or to anticipate future consequences. Although seeking an immediate resolution to an issue may appear easier in some circumstances, in other cases it is important to be patient and try to think ahead. Often, good things will come to those who wait, and someone with long-term vision and drive is more likely to achieve great things.

The ear hurts

MIMI GA ITAI

耳が痛い

It is not pleasant to hear someone itemizing your weaknesses and mistakes, and in Japan, it is said to 'hurt your ears'. Whether about your habits, your work ethic or just the way you handle life, when a comment touches a nerve, it can be upsetting. We all have things about ourselves that we would like to change, but that doesn't make it any less painful when someone points them out. In fact, we may be in denial and feel exposed and ashamed that someone else recognizes what we have refused to acknowledge. In Japanese, that makes 'your ears hurt'.

Teeth don't stand

HA GA TATANAI

歯が立たない

立たない / *tatanai* / literally means 'something does not stand', in this case referring to your teeth. Just as your teeth cannot stand upright on their own, 歯が立たない / *ha ga tatanai* / is used to describe a situation which is beyond your power to handle. So when you struggle but fail to beat your opponent in a sports match, or to figure out the answers in a maths exam, you can say, 'my teeth don't stand' – it was beyond me.

To make the
neck long

KUBI O NAGAKU SURU

首を長くする

How do you feel when you are waiting
impatiently for something? Whether you
are waiting for important exam results, or
anticipating the day when you can finally see
your long-distance partner, in Japanese this
feeling is described as 'waiting while making
the neck long', as it so neatly describes that
feeling of stretching your neck and looking
around with eager anticipation. Even though
the idiom itself implies that you are waiting,
it often goes together with the separate
verb 待つ / *matsu* / to wait, and the phrase
首を長くして待つ / *kubi o nagaku shite matsu* /
which literally means 'to make the neck long
and wait'.

The hand comes out of the throat

NODO KARA TE GA DERU

喉から手が出る

When you desperately want something, you may exaggerate and say that your hand is coming out of your throat to grab the thing that you desire! You could be longing for something rare and expensive; in other words, something that is out of your reach for the moment. The full sentence would be 喉から手が出るほど欲しい / *nodo kara te ga deru hodo hoshii* / meaning, 'I want this so much that my hand comes out of my throat'.

To hold one's shoulder

KATA O MOTSU

肩
を
持
つ

Have you ever found yourself in a position where two of your friends are having an argument and you find yourself taking somebody's side? That is what the Japanese call 'to hold a shoulder'. 肩を持つ / *kata o motsu* / refers to taking sides by agreeing with or defending one side of a conflict, no matter which side of the argument is more legitimate. For that reason, you may get into an awkward situation where a person gets upset and asks: 'Why do you hold his shoulder, not mine?'

To stretch out one's chest

MUNE O HARU

胸を張る

You can show your confidence and energy by 'stretching out your chest'. This idiom is often used as encouragement for someone who is entering a competition, playing in a sports match or taking an important exam. For example, you might say: 胸を張って頑張って！/ *mune o hatte ganbatte!* / 'stretch your chest and do your best!' Even if you are not feeling particularly confident, adopting this posture may give you the energy you need to perform to the best of your ability.

The stomach stands

HARA GA TATSU

腹が立つ

Getting angry is said to make your 'stomach stand' in Japanese. In this expression, the stomach actually signifies your heart. When your heartbeat quickens, it feels like it stands up inside your belly. The verb 立つ/ *tatsu* / literally means to stand, but it also describes the state of being more dynamic and less stable.

The waist is heavy

KOSHI GA OMOI

腰が重い

You may say that you feel your waist is heavy when you are not motivated to do a boring task or go to a party that you don't particularly want to attend. The weight makes you sluggish and slow to act. This is when you are not in the mood for doing anything other than collapsing into a comfortable couch. Your waist then becomes so heavy that you cannot stand up.

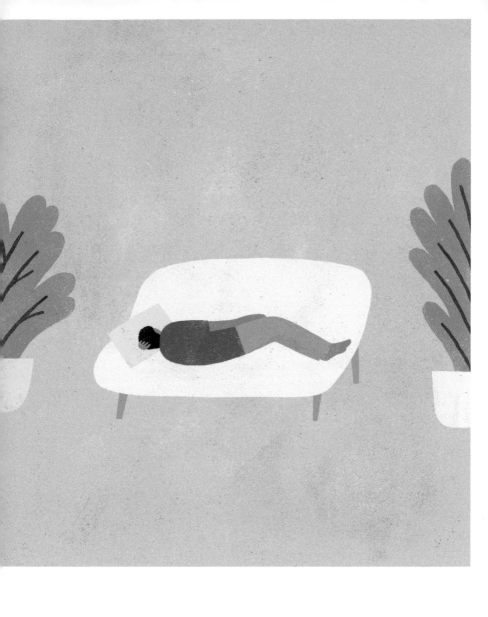

To carry the feet

ASHI O HAKOBU

足を運ぶ

In Japanese, you can say you carry your feet when you take the trouble to pay a visit somewhere. It might be a concert, museum, party or anywhere you plan to go. Instead of simply saying 行く / *iku* / which means to go, 足を運ぶ /*ashi o hakobu* / means going somewhere that takes some additional effort on your part.

To hang on
the crotch

MATA NI KAKERU

股に掛ける

When someone is travelling back and forth between different countries for work or other reasons, the Japanese call it 'hanging a bridge on one's crotch'. Figuratively, this is like spreading one's legs to form a bridge between two or more places. If you often go on international business trips, or if you are an artist who travels the world to perform, people will say that you 世界を股に掛けて活躍している / *sekai o mata ni kakete katsuyaku shiteiru* / are doing a fantastic job worldwide – literally, that you are forming bridges to countries all over the world!

It doesn't fall into one's guts

FU NI OCHINAI

腑に落ちない

When Japanese people are not convinced by something, that is because the story or the situation 'doesn't fall into their guts'. You can also use this idiom when you are not happy with the result of something. For example, your colleague got a promotion even though you don't think they deserve it – then this doesn't really fall into your guts!

The horse is a match

UMA GA AU

馬が合う

Horse riders and their mounts have to be in perfect unison to ensure a good race. They have to trust and understand each other. With people, too – whether the relationship is romantic, friendly or professional – you are more likely to build a sustainable and enjoyable relationship with someone whose vision and nature match yours.

I wish to borrow even a cat's paw

NEKO NO TE MO KARITAI

When you have a lot on your plate, you may want a little help from someone. This expression indicates that you're so busy that you'd even welcome the help of a cat (despite the fact that cats are unlikely to be of any use at all). One thing you need to be aware of with this idiom, however, is that you should never say it directly to someone. For example, saying: 'Could you give me a hand because I am so busy that I would even appreciate a cat's paw at the moment!' would be considered very impolite!

猫の手も借りたい

Even cats and rice ladles

NEKO MO SHAKUSHI MO

猫も杓子も

You may know what 猫 / *neko* / means – cat! But what about 杓子 / *shakushi* /? *Shakushi* is an ancient Japanese term for a rice paddle or ladle; known as 杓文字 / *shamoji* / in modern Japanese. Both cats and rice ladles are very common in Japan, so the expression simply means 'everyone'. There are many explanations as to why rice ladles became part of this saying. One of the best-known is that it came from the phrase 女子も弱子も / *meko mo jakushi mo* / meaning women and children. At some time in the distant past, 女子 / *meko* / women, was misheard as 猫 / *neko* / cat, and 弱子 / *jakushi* / children, as 杓子 / *shakushi* / ride ladle. This was then passed down through generations until the original meaning was lost. In any case, cats and rice ladles are now known to represent everybody – like 'every Tom, Dick and Harry'.

To read mackerel

SABA O YOMU

鯖を読む

Mackerel is a fish that spoils very quickly when in contact with the air, so you must be very quick to count them at the fish market. For that reason, there can be discrepancies between the actual number of fish and the number reported. When someone is not being completely honest with numbers – for instance when lying about their age – the Japanese say they are 'reading mackerel', and falsifying numbers for their own advantage.

Little fish grinding their teeth

GOMAME NO HAGISHIRI

ごまめの歯ぎしり

ごまめ / *gomame* / is a tiny dried Japanese anchovy often served as part of a new year celebration meal. In this expression, the fish represent something trivial or of no consequence – people of no particular ability. If little fish try to grind their teeth – or someone with no ability tries hard to achieve something without success and feels bitter about it – it has little or no impact on the rest of the world.

The fish that you lost seems greater than it is

NOGASHITA SAKANA WA OOKII

逃した魚は大きい

Imagine you are fishing and about to catch the biggest fish you have ever seen. But after a long struggle, the fish manages to escape and swims away from you. You are frustrated. You tell your friends about it, think it over all night long over the following days, and the fish gradually becomes far more significant than it should. This is human nature: the things that we cannot get or could not keep always seem to be the most valuable. It can also be applied to people. When we take something or someone for granted, we regret it all the more when they are gone.

Even monkeys can fall down from trees

SARU MO KI KARA OCHIRU

猿も木から落ちる

Even though monkeys are the world's greatest tree climbers, they are still susceptible to making a mistake that would send them straight to the ground. In other words, even the experts fail at times. On a personal level, it means that it is okay to make mistakes as long as we can learn from them.

To swallow like a cormorant

UNOMI NI SURU

鵜呑みにする

'

We live in a world where we are constantly bombarded with information, whether from the media or people around us. For that reason, it is essential to learn how to think critically and understand whose agenda that information is serving. When someone merely believes what they are being told without question, the Japanese say they 'swallow like a cormorant', because when a cormorant catches its prey, it simply swallows it whole, without chewing it up first.

A word from the crane

TSURU NO HITOKOE

鶴の一声

With their long necks, elongated bodies and high-pitched shrieks, cranes could be considered among the most intimidating birds in the animal kingdom. Because of this, they are often associated with figures of dominance and authority – typically heads of families or members of company management. A single word from the crane has the power to settle any troublesome situation, restore order and resolve ongoing arguments.

A line like a long snake

CHOODA NO RETSU

長蛇の列

In Japan, it is common to see disciplined queues of people waiting in seemingly endless lines to eat the best ramen in town, purchase their favourite band's new merchandise or buy the latest iPhone. (Of course, this phenomenon has a lot to do with the population density in big cities.) Those lines are sometimes so long that they look like a huge snake stretching around the streets.

The moon and a soft-shell turtle

TSUKI TO SUPPON

月とスッポン

How do you compare the moon and a soft-shell turtle? About the only thing they have in common is that they are both roughly spherical. The moon shines with its silver light in the night sky, while the soft-shell turtle is said to crawl around in the mud and obstinately hang on to anything it bites. This idiom highlights the fact that these two things represent such extremes that they cannot be talked about in the same breath, like chalk and cheese.

Dumplings
over flowers

HANA YORI DANGO

花
よ
り
団
子

This expression compares and contrasts
two symbolic objects – rice-cake dumplings
and flowers. Dumplings represent practical
essentials; flowers symbolize beauty. The
Japanese expression suggests that we
should always choose dumplings over
cherry blossom, pudding before praise or
bread rather than bird song – in other words
'substance over style'. In reality, of course,
both 花 / hana / and 団子 / dango / are
essential to our balanced well-being and are
inextricably linked, so the idiom cannot always
be taken literally and must be used carefully.
Depending on the context, it can convey,
on the one hand, a note of self-mockery or,
on the other, direct a laugh at those who do
not understand the elegance and beauty of
the world around them.

Packed
like sushi

SUSHI ZUME

すしづめ

Sushi is a delicate food and must be packed into its box tightly, as any gaps can cause it to fall apart. The scene in a central Tokyo commuter train is often described as / すしづめ / *sushi zume* /. Big department store sales also tend to get shoppers in a state of *sushi zume*. A more sinister use of the expression would be to describe the experience of evacuating from a disaster that has forced people to stay in a confined space, packed in tightly.

About the author

Yoshie Omata was born and raised in Yamanashi, Japan, in a city known for its beautiful view of Fuji-san, where she developed a love of languages and music. After studying in England for her Master's degree, she worked in the arts and culture industry and later became a certified Japanese language tutor, translator, and content creator (@japanesewithyoshie). She also speaks English and is actively learning French.

Acknowledgments

First and foremost, I would like to express my deepest gratitude to my parents, who have always been supportive of my decisions at every stage of my life. I wouldn't have been here today without their kindness and the generous support. Thank you so much, mum and dad. I am forever grateful to have been born as your daughter.

I would also like to thank my lovely husband, Eric. He is my motivation to keep learning, stay positive, and trust myself. *Merci* Eric, you make my every day brighter and better.

To my wonderful friends, students, and work partners, thank you for your support and for being a source of inspiration.

I extend my sincere gratitude to Sofie Shearman from Quadrille, for finding me on the vast internet universe and giving me this extraordinary opportunity to write a book. I would never have imagined myself being a book author. Thank you so much, Sofie, Stacey, Katherine, and everyone at Quadrille. I would like to dedicate one of my favourite Japanese idioms to you. I did not include it in this book but it is this: 一期一会 – 'Once-in-a-lifetime encounter' – cherish each passing moment in order to live meaningfully.

MANAGING DIRECTOR
Sarah Lavelle

COMMISSIONING
EDITOR
Stacey Cleworth

ASSISTANT EDITOR
Sofie Shearman

WORDS
Yoshie Omata

JAPANESE EDITOR
Ayana Homma

DESIGN MANAGER
Katherine Case

ILLUSTRATOR
Nastia Sleptsova

SENIOR
PRODUCTION
CONTROLLER
Sabeena Atchia

Published in 2023 by Quadrille,
an imprint of Hardie Grant

Quadrille
52–54 Southwark Street
London SE1 1UN
quadrille.com

Cataloguing in Publication Data:
a catalogue record for this book is
available from the British Library.

ISBN 9781837830671
Printed in China